D1069052

STATE PROFILES

OREGON

BY PATRICK PERISH

BELLWETHER MEDIA • MINNEAPOLIS, MN

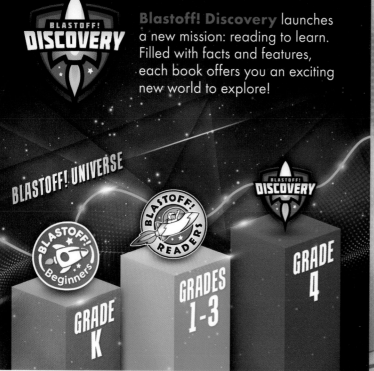

Blastoff! Discovery launches a new mission: reading to learn. Filled with facts and features, each book offers you an exciting new world to explore!

BLASTOFF! UNIVERSE

BLASTOFF! Beginners — GRADE K

BLASTOFF! READERS — GRADES 1-3

BLASTOFF! DISCOVERY — GRADE 4

This edition first published in 2022 by Bellwether Media, Inc.

No part of this publication may be reproduced in whole or in part without written permission of the publisher.
For information regarding permission, write to Bellwether Media, Inc., Attention: Permissions Department,
6012 Blue Circle Drive, Minnetonka, MN 55343.

Library of Congress Cataloging-in-Publication Data

Names: Perish, Patrick, author.
Title: Oregon / by Patrick Perish.
Description: Minneapolis, MN : Bellwether Media, Inc., 2022. |
    Series: Blastoff! Discovery: State profiles | Includes bibliographical
    references and index. | Audience: Ages 7-13 | Audience: Grades
    4-6 | Summary: "Engaging images accompany information about
    Oregon. The combination of high-interest subject matter and
    narrative text is intended for students in grades 3 through 8"–
    Provided by publisher.
Identifiers: LCCN 2021019695 (print) | LCCN 2021019696 (ebook)
    | ISBN 9781644873427 (library binding) |
    ISBN 9781648341854 (ebook)
Subjects: LCSH: Oregon–Juvenile literature.
Classification: LCC F876.3 .P47 2022 (print) | LCC F876.3 (ebook)
    | DDC 979.5–dc23
LC record available at https://lccn.loc.gov/2021019695
LC ebook record available at https://lccn.loc.gov/2021019696

Editor: Colleen Sexton   Designer: Andrea Schneider

Printed in the United States of America, North Mankato, MN.

TABLE OF CONTENTS

Two hikers trek through a forest of pines and firs. They climb to a lookout and take in a sweeping view. Rocky cliffs circle the deep-blue waters of **Crater** Lake. The crater is part of an ancient **volcano**. It caved in 7,700 years ago. Rain and snow filled the bowl-shaped crater, making the lake.

DEEP BLUE

Crater Lake lies in Oregon's Cascade Mountains. It is the deepest lake in the United States. It reaches 1,943 feet (592 meters) deep!

WIZARD ISLAND
CRATER LAKE

CANNON BEACH

COLUMBIA RIVER GORGE

HELLS CANYON

PAINTED HILLS

The hikers spy Wizard Island rising from the lake. It is the top of a small volcano. They follow a steep path down to the lake. They swim and fish for trout. Back on shore, they spot the rare Crater Lake newt. Welcome to Oregon!

N
W + E
S

Oregon is in the **Pacific Northwest** region of the United States. The Columbia River forms the state's northern border with Washington. The Snake River separates Oregon from Idaho to the east. Nevada and California border Oregon to the south. The Pacific Ocean washes the state's western coast.

Oregon covers 98,379 square miles (254,800 square kilometers). The Cascade Mountains run north to south through the middle of Oregon. There, Mount Hood rises to the highest point in the state. Salem is the capital of Oregon. It sits in northwestern Oregon in the Willamette Valley. Other major cities include Portland, Eugene, and Bend.

PACIFIC OCEAN

A GREAT GORGE

The Snake River carved Hells Canyon. This narrow passage has steep walls. It is the deepest river gorge in North America!

WASHINGTON

COLUMBIA
RIVER

PORTLAND

SALEM

SNAKE
RIVER

BEND

EUGENE

OREGON

IDAHO

CALIFORNIA

NEVADA

THE LEWIS AND CLARK EXPEDITION

People first arrived in Oregon about 12,000 years ago. Over time, they formed Native American communities. Tribes included the Chinook, Kalapuya, and Paiute. Spanish and British explorers reached the coast in the 1500s. In 1805, Meriwether Lewis and William Clark led an **expedition** that crossed Oregon. Fur traders established Astoria in 1811.

In the 1830s, **pioneers** from the eastern United States began traveling to Oregon. Their 2,000-mile (3,219-kilometer) route became known as the Oregon Trail. Conflicts occurred as these people moved onto Native American lands. Oregon became the 33rd state in 1859. By 1883, the U.S. government had forced most tribes onto **reservations**.

NATIVE PEOPLES OF OREGON

PAIUTE, WARM SPRINGS, AND WASCO

- Original lands in central and southern Oregon
- About 3,500 are on the Burns Paiute Indian Colony and the Warm Springs Indian Reservation today

UMATILLA, CAYUSE, AND WALLA WALLA

- Original lands along the Columbia River in northern Oregon
- About 3,000 are on the Umatilla Reservation today

COOS, LOWER UMPQUA, AND SIUSLAW

- Original lands along the western coast of Oregon
- About 1,200 in Oregon today

KLAMATH, MODOC, AND YAHOOSKIN

- Original lands in the Klamath Basin of south-central Oregon and northern California
- About 5,200 in Oregon today

In western Oregon, rocky shores and sandy beaches meet the low mountains of the Coast Range. Just east, a broad valley of rich farmland surrounds the Willamette River. The forested Cascade Mountains tower over the valley's eastern side. The Klamath Mountains rise on the southwestern border. Eastern Oregon is part of the Columbia **Plateau**. River **gorges** and mountains break up this flat stretch of land. Grasses and brush grow in the dry landscape of the southeast.

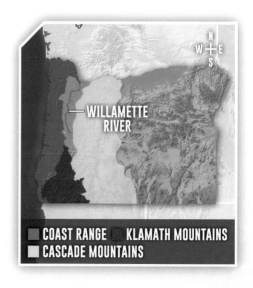

—WILLAMETTE RIVER

■ COAST RANGE ■ KLAMATH MOUNTAINS
■ CASCADE MOUNTAINS

OREGON COAST AND COAST RANGE

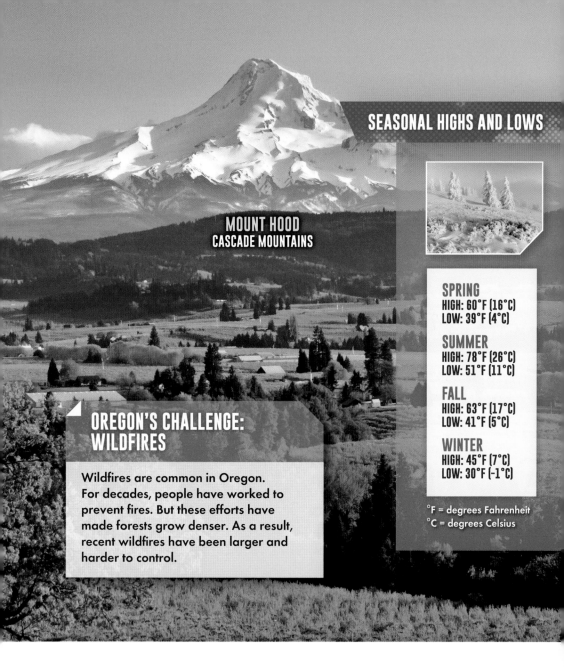

MOUNT HOOD
CASCADE MOUNTAINS

SPRING
HIGH: 60°F (16°C)
LOW: 39°F (4°C)

SUMMER
HIGH: 78°F (26°C)
LOW: 51°F (11°C)

FALL
HIGH: 63°F (17°C)
LOW: 41°F (5°C)

WINTER
HIGH: 45°F (7°C)
LOW: 30°F (-1°C)

°F = degrees Fahrenheit
°C = degrees Celsius

OREGON'S CHALLENGE: WILDFIRES

Wildfires are common in Oregon. For decades, people have worked to prevent fires. But these efforts have made forests grow denser. As a result, recent wildfires have been larger and harder to control.

Western Oregon has mild winters and cool summers. Ocean winds often bring rain. The area east of the Cascades is drier. There, winters are cold and summers are hot.

AMERICAN BEAVER

Oregon's forests, waters, and mountains provide habitats for wildlife. Beavers repair their dams in streams, while elk gather to drink nearby. Black bears and scrub jays gobble berries in thorny thickets. In the shade of Douglas firs, banana slugs ooze over golden mushrooms. Pronghorn race through eastern grasslands. On rocky slopes, furry pikas gather plants to store for winter. They watch out for hungry hawks.

ELK

Sea lions rest along rocky ocean shores. **Tide pools** catch sea stars and sea urchins. In coastal waters, Dungeness crabs hide in eelgrass beds. Salmon swim up cold rivers from the sea to lay their eggs.

BANANA SLUGS

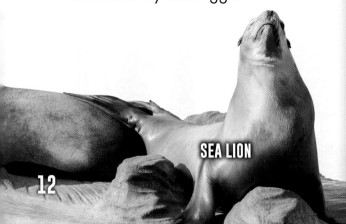

SEA LION

AMERICAN PIKA

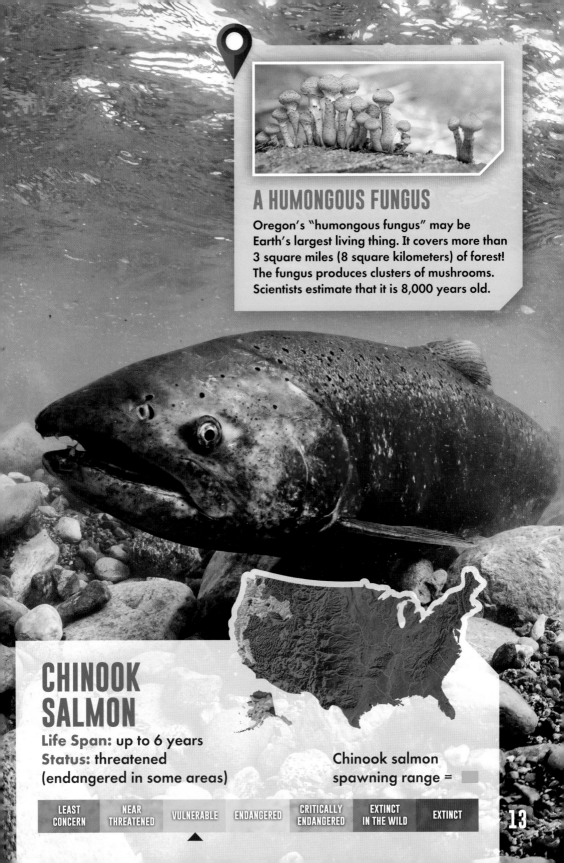

A HUMONGOUS FUNGUS

Oregon's "humongous fungus" may be Earth's largest living thing. It covers more than 3 square miles (8 square kilometers) of forest! The fungus produces clusters of mushrooms. Scientists estimate that it is 8,000 years old.

CHINOOK SALMON

Life Span: up to 6 years
Status: threatened (endangered in some areas)

Chinook salmon spawning range =

LEAST CONCERN	NEAR THREATENED	VULNERABLE	ENDANGERED	CRITICALLY ENDANGERED	EXTINCT IN THE WILD	EXTINCT

About 4.2 million people call Oregon home. Around four of every five Oregonians live near cities. The largest population centers are in the Willamette Valley. This region drew travelers on the Oregon Trail. Eastern Oregon is largely **rural**.

EUGENE
WILLAMETTE VALLEY

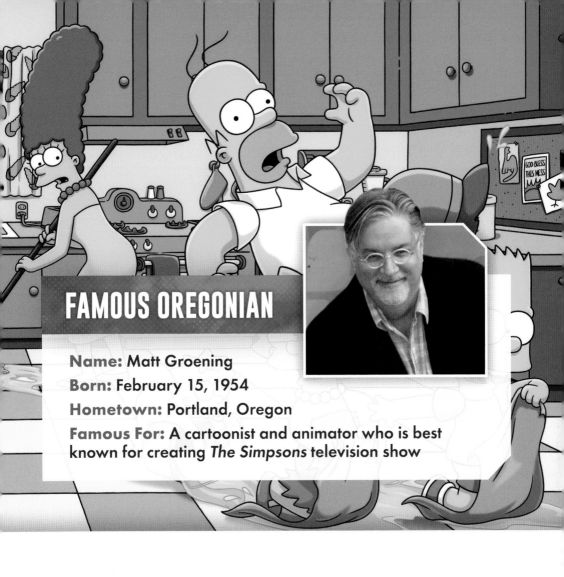

FAMOUS OREGONIAN

Name: Matt Groening
Born: February 15, 1954
Hometown: Portland, Oregon
Famous For: A cartoonist and animator who is best known for creating *The Simpsons* television show

Oregonians come from many different backgrounds. Most have **ancestors** from Germany, England, Norway, and other European countries. About 1 in 10 residents is Hispanic. Small numbers of Oregonians are Black or African American. Some Asian Americans also live in the state. The state is also home to nine federally recognized Native American tribes. Around 1 of every 10 Oregonians is an **immigrant**. Most newcomers come from Mexico, Vietnam, China, and India.

Founded in 1845, Portland is Oregon's largest city. It sits in the northwest where the Willamette and Columbia Rivers meet. Timber and farm products launched the city's shipping industry. Today, Portland is a major port and a center for tech.

A WILD RIDE!

Thousands turn out every year for the Portland Adult Soapbox Derby. People ride wacky homemade carts down Mount Tabor. Prizes are awarded for looks and speed.

Portland is nicknamed the City of Roses for its many rose gardens. It is also known for being bike-friendly. Bike paths crisscross the city. Hikers enjoy Forest Park. It is one of the country's largest **urban** forests. Washington Park features a Japanese garden, a zoo, and a children's museum. Residents also enjoy local ballet, orchestra, and theater performances.

INTERNATIONAL ROSE
TEST GARDEN
WASHINGTON PARK

INDUSTRY

Oregon has a wealth of **natural resources**. The state is a top producer of blueberries, blackberries, hazelnuts, and flower bulbs. Farmers grow wheat and raise cattle in eastern Oregon. Fishing crews haul in salmon and rockfish. Forests cover almost half the state. They make Oregon a leading producer of lumber and other forest products.

OREGON'S CHALLENGE: DAMS

Oregon's river dams create clean, low-cost electricity. But they also threaten salmon habitats. The dams block salmon from swimming to areas where they lay their eggs. Balancing energy needs with the salmon population is an ongoing challenge in Oregon.

Paper mills and wood-processing plants are major **manufacturing** industries. Factory workers also make electronics and computer parts. Beaverton is the home of footwear and clothing company Nike. Most Oregonians have **service jobs**. They work in hospitals, banks, and stores. **Tourism** also employs many service workers.

INVENTED IN OREGON

SAF-SKI SAFE-RELEASE SKI BINDINGS

Date Invented: 1937

Inventor: Hjalmar Hvam

PHILLIPS-HEAD SCREW AND SCREWDRIVER

Date Invented: 1932

Inventor: John P. Thompson

TATER TOTS

Date Invented: 1953

Inventors: F. Nephi Grigg and Golden Grigg

WIKIS (CROWD-EDITED ARTICLES)

Date Invented: 1995

Inventor: Ward Cunningham

19

MARIONBERRY
COBBLER

Oregon's **farmers markets** offer locally produced foods. Marionberries feature in pies, shakes, and other desserts. Oregon's dairy farms and **creameries** make world-champion blue cheeses. Cooks use wild mushrooms in creamy risottos and rich soups. Gardenburgers consisting of rice, oats, and mushrooms were first made in Oregon. Oregonians also enjoy roasted hazelnuts.

THE NOSE KNOWS

Truffles are among the most highly prized mushrooms in the world. At the Oregon Truffle Festival, dogs are trained to sniff out these valuable wild foods.

Portland's food trucks carry hearty meals to go. They serve up Korean barbecue, wood-fired pizzas, and other flavorful dishes. Crab legs and fish and chips are popular along the coast. Many Native Americans honor the year's first salmon catch. They bake it over wood fires for community celebrations.

WOOD-FIRED PIZZA

CRAB LEGS

OREGON HAZELNUT TRAIL MIX

ABOUT 10 CUPS

Have an adult help you make this yummy treat!

INGREDIENTS

6 cups Kix cereal

1 1/2 cups coarsely chopped or whole roasted hazelnuts

1 cup golden raisins

1 cup banana chips

1 small package non-instant vanilla pudding

1/2 cup honey

1/2 cup peanut butter

DIRECTIONS

1. Mix the cereal, nuts, raisins, and banana chips together.

2. In a saucepan, combine the vanilla pudding and honey. Bring to a boil and boil for 30 seconds.

3. Remove from heat. Stir in the peanut butter and mix well.

4. Pour over the cereal mixture and mix until it is coated. Put the mix on a cookie sheet to cool.

There is always something fun to do in the Beaver State. Hikers and bikers explore the state's many trails and parks. Mountain climbers take on the rocky slopes of the Cascades. Hunters pursue deer, elk, and game birds. Sports fans cheer for the Portland Timbers and Portland Thorns soccer teams. The Portland Trail Blazers basketball team also draws huge crowds.

Oregon has a thriving arts community. Residents enjoy live music and theater. The world-renowned Oregon Shakespeare Festival is in Ashland. More than 700 performances each year bring to life Shakespearean and modern plays. Talented Oregonians also show off their work at art fairs.

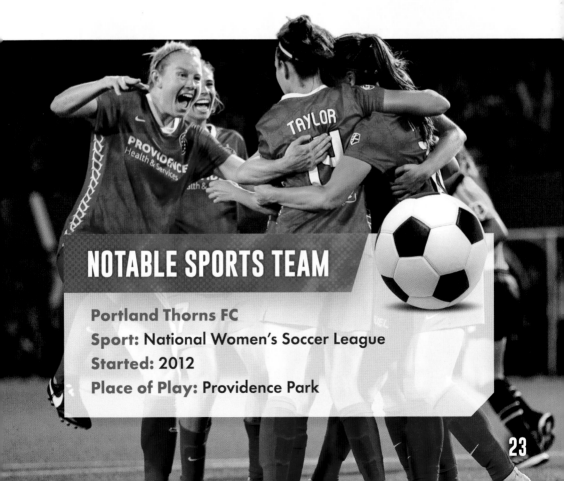

NOTABLE SPORTS TEAM

Portland Thorns FC
Sport: National Women's Soccer League
Started: 2012
Place of Play: Providence Park

Festivals bring Oregonians together. Siletz hosts the annual Nesika Illahee **Pow Wow** in August. Visitors can experience **traditional** Native American dances and food. June's Portland Rose Festival is over 100 years old. It features decorated parade floats and teams paddling in dragon boat races. The Oregon Country Fair draws crowds to Veneta each July. It celebrates living in harmony with nature.

The Cannon Beach Sandcastle Contest is fun in the sun. Sandcastle artists sculpt fantastic figures and scenes. The Pickathon Music Festival in Happy Valley brings together a wide variety of musicians. There is plenty to celebrate in Oregon!

PICKATHON MUSIC FESTIVAL

CANNON BEACH
SANDCASTLE CONTEST

25

1859

Oregon becomes the 33rd state

1500s

About 125 Native American tribes live in the region when Spanish and English explorers sail along the Pacific coast

1811

The Pacific Fur Company founds Astoria, the first white settlement in what is now Oregon

1805

The Lewis and Clark expedition reaches the mouth of the Columbia River

1830s

Thousands of pioneers begin traveling on the Oregon Trail

1912

Oregon gives women
the right to vote

1980

Mount St. Helens in
Washington erupts, causing
layers of ash to fall on Oregon

1933

Construction begins
on the Bonneville
Dam located on the
Columbia River

2015

Oregon becomes
the first state to
automatically
enroll voters

1883

The U.S. government has forced
most Native Americans off of
their land in Oregon

Nickname: The Beaver State

Motto: *Alis volat propriis*
(She flies with her own wings)

Date of Statehood: February 14, 1859
(the 33rd state)

Capital City: Salem ⭐

Other Major Cities: Portland, Eugene, Bend

Area: 98,379 square miles (254,800 square kilometers);
Oregon is the 9th largest state.

Population

4,237,256
(2020)

STATE FLAG

front

back

Adopted in 1925, Oregon's state flag is blue and has designs on both sides. The front has the state name, the year of statehood, and an eagle perched atop a shield. Symbols on the shield represent Oregon's natural resources, history, and industry. They include a forest, a covered wagon, and a ship on the Pacific Ocean. Thirty-three stars surrounding the shield show that Oregon is the 33rd state. A beaver appears on the back of the flag.

INDUSTRY

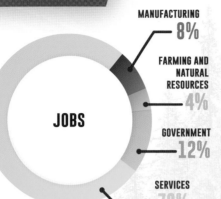

MANUFACTURING
8%

FARMING AND NATURAL RESOURCES
4%

JOBS

GOVERNMENT
12%

SERVICES
76%

Main Exports

computer and electronic parts

machine parts

chemicals

aircraft and parts

wheat

Natural Resources
timber, soil, water, mineral deposits

GOVERNMENT

8 ELECTORAL VOTES

Federal Government
6 | 2
REPRESENTATIVES | SENATORS

USA

OR

State Government
60 | 30
REPRESENTATIVES | SENATORS

STATE SYMBOLS

STATE FISH
CHINOOK SALMON

STATE ANIMAL
BEAVER

STATE MUSHROOM
PACIFIC GOLDEN CHANTERELLE

STATE TREE
DOUGLAS FIR

GLOSSARY

ancestors—relatives who lived long ago

crater—the bowl-shaped opening of a volcano

creameries—places where milk is made into other products, such as cream and cheese

expedition—a journey with a purpose, such as to explore an area

farmers markets—markets where local farmers sell goods

gorges—narrow canyons with steep walls

immigrant—someone who moves to a new country

manufacturing—a field of work in which people use machines to make products

natural resources—materials in the earth that are taken out and used to make products or fuel

Pacific Northwest—an area of the United States that includes Washington, Oregon, and Idaho

pioneers—people who are among the first to explore or settle in an area

plateau—an area of flat, raised land

pow wow—a Native American gathering that usually includes dancing

reservations—areas of land that are controlled by Native American tribes

rural—related to the countryside

service jobs—jobs that perform tasks for people or businesses

tide pools—pools of ocean water left when the tide goes out

tourism—the business of people traveling to visit other places

traditional—related to customs, ideas, or beliefs handed down from one generation to the next

urban—related to cities and city life

volcano—a hole in the earth; when a volcano erupts, hot ash, gas, or melted rock called lava shoots out.

AT THE LIBRARY

Blashfield, Jean F. *The Amazing Lewis and Clark Expedition*. North Mankato, Minn.: Capstone Press, 2018.

Gregory, Josh. *Oregon*. New York, N.Y.: Children's Press, 2019.

Hamilton, John. *Oregon: The Beaver State*. Minneapolis, Minn.: Abdo and Daughters, 2017.

ON THE WEB

FACTSURFER

Factsurfer.com gives you a safe, fun way to find more information.

1. Go to www.factsurfer.com.

2. Enter "Oregon" into the search box and click 🔍.

3. Select your book cover to see a list of related content.

INDEX